IMAGES
of America

MAINE LIFE

AT THE TURN OF THE CENTURY
THROUGH THE PHOTOGRAPHS OF
NETTIE CUMMINGS MAXIM

WALTER & WINNIE, DAISY FIELD (1909). This image of Walter and Winnie Maxim picking daisies in a field above the farm is, without doubt, Nettie Maxim's most popular photograph. The woods in the background have long since swallowed up this spectacular field and the daisies have vanished.

FRONT COVER ILLUSTRATION: EATING WATERMELON (SEE P. 88).

IMAGES
of America

MAINE LIFE

AT THE TURN OF THE CENTURY
THROUGH THE PHOTOGRAPHS OF
NETTIE CUMMINGS MAXIM

Diane and Jack Barnes

ARCADIA

First published 1995
Copyright © Diane and Jack Barnes, 1995

ISBN 0-7524-0240-4

Published by Arcadia Publishing,
an imprint of the Chalford Publishing Corporation
One Washington Center, Dover, New Hampshire 03820
Printed in Great Britain

Library of Congress Cataloging-in-Publication Data applied for

FAMILY PICNIC, ICE CAVES (1906). The Maxims and Cummings enjoying a picnic at the Greenwood Ice Caves in the summer of 1906. From right to left are Walter Maxim, Earle Maxim, Winnie Maxim, Inez Bean Cummings, Frances Cummings, Florence Cummings, and Eugene Cummings. Moses Cummings is in the background.

Contents

Acknowledgments

We wish to express our profound appreciation to the many individuals whose invaluable contributions made this project possible. First of all we are deeply grateful to Nettie Cummings Maxim's two children, Winnie and Walter, for preserving and donating their mother's glass negatives to the Greenwood Historical Society and willingly giving their time for interviews. We only regret that they both had passed away before we undertook this project. The response of Nettie's surviving descendants has been simply amazing. Family photo albums, sundry memorabilia, and fascinating tidbits of information flowed in from many directions. For example, her grandson, Edgar Merrill (who lives on a farm in Waterford), her granddaughter, Marilyn Maxim Wilson (from San Antonio, Texas), and her great-granddaughter, Peggy Poskus (of East Islip, New York) generously loaned us precious images appearing in this work. Without the Greenwood Historical Society and the many hours of hard work on the part of Blaine Mills and Margaret Mills, this project would never have gotten off the ground. We also wish to thank Randall H. Bennet and Stanley R. Howe of the Bethel Historical Society, Ben B. Conant of South Paris, Mansfield Packard (who grew up on Bird Hill and worked on the Maxim Farm), Richard Fraser, and Jane Sumner.

NETTIE B CUMMINGS

PEN-AND-INK DRAWING. Nettie's innate love for flowers is exemplified in this pen-and-ink drawing done in 1891 on the inside cover of her algebra book at Gould Academy.

Introduction

Nettie Cummings Maxim (1876–1910) was the daughter of a farmer, married a farmer, and reared three children, two of whom lived out most of their long lives on farms. But unlike other young women in her area, many of whom were probably endowed with latent talents, her innate creative and artistic talent surfaced to be expressed through the lenses of her cameras. Between the years 1895 and 1910, she owned three of these.

There were other contemporary women photographers in Maine, and some have been published. What is unique about Nettie and her work is that she lived her life almost entirely on a farm on Bird Hill in the Oxford County town of Bethel and seldom ventured more than a few miles beyond Bird Hill. The real impact of her work is that she chronicled on film activities of a rather typical Maine hill farm and farming community, which included people, animals, buildings, the narrow, winding road leading up the hill, and landscapes throughout the four seasons. Then, too, she took many valuable photographs of the thriving village of Locke's Mills in the town of Greenwood, the economic, social, and service hub for the ten families who lived just a mile or so away on Bird Hill.

Not too long after the construction of the railroad, the scenic beauty of the area began attracting summer people; and a new dimension was added to this rural area. Nettie seems to have mingled quite successfully with many of the summer visitors and recorded the early development of the Greenwood area in terms of tourism.

Unquestionably Nettie was endowed with an innate artistic talent, and she did some painting and drawing. Thus it is not surprising that the preponderance of her photographs appear to be taken through the eyes of an artist. At the turn of the century, film was not very sensitive, so the shutter had to remain open for a long time. The long exposures mandated for the most part that photographs be staged or posed. Otherwise, whatever was going on would be blurred. Nettie turned the process of carefully posing her subjects into an advantage, and somehow managed to create in her photographs the illusion of motion, so that people often appear to be in motion doing real things.

Nettie gave painstaking care to detail and would plan for months and even a year in advance to take certain photographs, particularly of people involved in seasonal activity. She invariably took a series of photographs of particular subjects and activities on the same day. She was especially adept at using both natural and artificial light to attain maximum effectiveness. She also very quickly manifested a clear understanding of the importance of composition in photography.

Only a relatively few of her photographs are known to have been taken indoors. Often her portraits were taken out by the barn where she tacked a canvas screen behind a platform that served as a studio. In some of her glass negatives the boards of the barn are visible beyond the edges of her canvas background, but this could be cropped in the development process.

For Nettie an additional impediment to quality photography was that she seems to have had a lens that had not been properly ground. It had a "hot spot" in the middle. Consequently, the lens drew most of its light into the center. There the picture is dark and sharp, but it gets lighter and less clear toward the outer edges. Therefore, for Nettie to get an even exposure, she had to do what is called "dodging" to slow the exposure at the center when developing her negatives. She had to dodge the center of the picture, using a piece of cotton or cardboard. It was a challenge and a credit to her technical skills. Fortunately, two of her children—Walter Maxim and Winifred Maxim Merrill—who were subjects in many of their mother's photographs, kept many of her negatives and original photographs, although it is claimed in the family that some youngsters played with and broke some.

Nevertheless, over seven hundred of her glass negatives survived many years of storage in Winnie's barn and Walter's woodshed; and before their demise, they donated them to the Greenwood Historical Society. Recently, some of Nettie's photographs not in the Greenwood collection have also surfaced.

It is very likely that these negatives would have continued to gather dust were it not for the fact that the Greenwood Historical Society is exceptionally well organized and keenly dedicated to preserving the memories of its past. Blaine Mills, local historian and Greenwood Historical Society photographer, assisted by his wife Margaret, has logged interminable hours in the workroom at the Society cleaning, labeling, numbering, and cataloging each of the negatives. The Society has a well-equipped darkroom with an antique Elwood enlarger that can handle glass negatives. Compounding their task, two additional cartons of negatives were uncovered after they were midway through the project. Other negatives, also, have trickled in from time to time, creating an even greater challenge to their organizational system. Then, too, it remained for them to identify as many as possible of the people, places, and even the names of cats and horses in the photographs.

Blaine's task was made easier, because he was able to interview Walter and Winifred many times before they died and consulted others who had either lived or worked at some point in their lives on Bird Hill before the landscape was drastically transformed.

Although most of the photographs in this collection are part of the Greenwood Historical Society's Maxim collection, some have been borrowed from family photograph albums. The titles on photographs included here are usually Nettie's. Specific dates are included whenever possible. The photographs in this collection are arranged in an effort to illustrate Maine at the turn of the century through the life and experiences of Nettie Maxim Cummings.

Through her cameras Nettie recorded a tiny piece of the world that was so endearing to her. In doing so, she has given immortality to people, buildings, and even animals that were a part of her life and her microcosm of society nearly a century ago. Although she did not photograph everything we would like to see, she did present us with precious vignettes of life in rural Maine at the turn of the century. The more we view her work, the more we learn.

EARLE AND HIS PASSENGERS. Earle Maxim seems to be enjoying giving these three little girls a ride in his wagon.

One
Nettie Cummings Maxim
and Her Photography

SELF-PORTRAIT. Nettie Cummings Maxim was born Nettie Belle Cummings on August 1, 1876, at the Maxim Farm on Bird Hill in Bethel, Maine. The daughter of a farmer, the wife of a farmer, and the mother of three children, Nettie seemed destined to go the way of the vast majority of farm women in rural Maine in her day—performing interminable mundane tasks with little or no contact with the outside world. But Nettie early in life evinced an innate artistic talent. Perhaps she would have captured the essence of her mini-world with a paintbrush on canvas in her spare time had she not become intrigued with photography and about 1895 acquired a small camera, possibly from a young and accomplished photographer in the area named Guy Coffin.

THE MAXIM FARM HOUSE. It was in this farmhouse on Bird Hill, called the old Abraham Jordan Place, that Nettie Belle Cummings was born. It was the house she grew up in and continued living in after her marriage. It was here that she gave birth to her three children, and it was here that she departed from this earth much too soon on May 29, 1910, when Bird Hill was redolent of the flowers and blossoms she loved to photograph.

One wonders how she ever found the time to take up photography since she had to devote so much of her time to preparing meals, preserving home-grown vegetables, fruits, and meats, nursing her husband and children in time of illness, and making and mending clothes for herself and the family. In summer, when she did much of her photography, she was burdened with having to stand over a hot wood stove cooking three meals a day for the large crew of farmhands who boarded at the farm during berry-picking time.

Of course, there was no electricity or other amenities which are commonplace throughout most of rural Maine today. Thus, for Nettie, developing her negatives had to have been a real challenge, and it is a credit to her mechanical aptitude that she did so well.

Her darkroom consisted of a closet which she locked herself in while developing her glass negatives. For light to work by, she used a kerosene lamp with a red chimney and red shade.

The technique for developing glass negatives in Nettie's day was called contact printing. She must have laid the photographic paper out in the darkroom and then placed her glass negative on top of the paper. With no electricity, she must have opened up the door and exposed the negative to the sunlight for a few seconds, thus giving an exact copy and size of the negative itself. Although enlargers were in use at the time Nettie did her photography, there is no evidence that she ever possessed one.

This picture of the Maxim farmhouse was taken by Nettie with her 1-1/2-by-2-inch format camera between 1895 and 1899. The glass negative is not known to exist. It was copied and enlarged from a small contact print that Nettie made. There are only thirty-four of these small negatives in the Greenwood Historical Society. Most of them are portraits.

10

GOULD ACADEMY (1909). After Nettie graduated from this highly-reputable academy in Bethel, founded in 1836, she taught school for a year in the neighboring town of Albany, now a plantation.

NETTIE BELLE AS A YOUNG GIRL. This portrait of Nettie was taken by Minnie Libby, a prominent professional photographer in her day, at her Cottage Studio in Norway. Sometime after Nettie took up photography, she copied this portrait of herself onto one of her glass negatives. It probably was taken at the time of her graduation from Gould Academy and seems to be the only extant portrait taken of her as a teenager.

NETTIE CUMMINGS MAXIM (1903–04). By the time Nettie took this self-portrait, she was a farmer's wife, the mother of three children, and clearly had become an accomplished photographer in an amazingly brief period of time, despite the exhausting demands that were made upon her on a daily basis.

What is most apparent is that her artistic talent transcended her photography. Here she is displaying her dexterity as a seamstress and evinces a proclivity for clothing design that is eye-catching and seems rather unique in rural Maine at the turn of the century. The abstract floral motif on her blouse suggests a Scandinavian or Finnish influence.

NETTIE'S 5-BY-7-INCH CAMERA. Sometime around 1900 Nettie acquired two cameras that were technically superior to the little 1-1/2-by-2-inch format that she had begun using in 1895. One was a 4-by-5-inch and the other a 5-by-7-inch format. Judging from the glass negatives that have survived, she seems to have used both simultaneously. Fortunately the latter remains in the family and could be photographed and identified, thanks to the George Eastman House in Rochester, New York.

Nettie's 5-by-7-inch format is a Tele-Photo Cycle Poco C camera that was first made by the Rochester Optical and Camera Company in 1900, a year after the company was formed, and could be purchased through mail order for approximately $25. The Cycle series of cameras was advertised to be carried around by one on a bicycle.

By 1903, however, cameras using glass plates were being replaced by film cameras, and the manufacturer of Nettie's camera sold out to George Eastman. Nettie, however, continued using her two cameras requiring glass plates for the remainder of her short life. (Glass plates were still available for her Poco C as late as 1950.)

The versatility of both of her newly acquired cameras is manifested in the remarkable detail and definition she was able to capture in her photographs. Her Poco C could accommodate lenses of any make and had a rack and pinion focusing attachment and a new swing back design that greatly enhanced its flexibility. She was able to capture in great detail her subjects in the foreground as well as a backdrop of undulating hills, the distant ponds, and the flocculent clouds floating in the sky over Bird Hill.

Nevertheless, her cameras lacked the flexibility of our modern day cameras; the emulsion speed of both was extremely slow, requiring that her subjects pose for each photograph. Yet, her subjects seem positively animated. There is a sense of motion in so many of her photographs. Little wonder that she was able to sell some of her photographs for postcards and thus can be considered at least a semi-professional photographer. Todd Gustavson of the George Eastman House said the use of the 5-by-7-inch format implies at least a more serious amateur.

NETTIE CUMMINGS MAXIM—A SELF-PORTRAIT. In this self-portrait, as well as in many of her portraits, she used a painted scenic canvas backing which she very often attached to the side of the Maxim barn. She is either holding behind her back the leather bellows that controlled the shutter or had someone—very likely one of her three children—take this photograph.

Interestingly she had only one tray containing flash powder for additional lighting. Therefore, the light all came from one side.

Two
The Family

CHILDREN IN THE SAND. The three Maxim children flash radiant smiles up at their mother's lens as they lie on the sand at the water's edge of one of the three ponds in Greenwood, about a mile down in the valley from their Bird Hill farm. From left to right are Walter Ellsworth (born November 16, 1897), Earle Leslie (born May 1, 1895), and Winifred Grace (born July 11, 1896). For Nettie, motherhood and photography seem to have bloomed simultaneously.

MOSES CUMMINGS. This photograph of Nettie's father was taken by an unknown photographer while he was serving in the Union Army during the Civil War. In 1903, she copied this portrait onto a 4-by-5-inch glass negative.

Moses was born on January 27, 1833, at Hamlin's Gore in Woodstock near the foot of Bird Hill—the son of Joseph Cummings and Cinderilla (Lapham) Cummings. His first wife, Julia E. Cummings, was from Bird Hill. The couple had two children—Eli Eugene and Emma Ellsworth.

Moses was twenty-eight years old when he enlisted in the Company B 3rd Maine Infantry soon after the outbreak of the Civil War and was later transferred to Company B 17th Maine. As a division teamster he drove a six-mule team transporting ammunition and supplies. He first saw action at the Second Battle of Bull Run, August 29, 1862.

The following winter he received the tragic news that his wife had passed away. He applied for a hardship leave, but his request was denied and his two children, Eli Eugene and Emma Ellsworth, were taken in by relatives.

Moses endured many hardships during the remainder of the war, which included being hospitalized in 1864 with yellow fever and being wounded in the hip. He served in Sherman's Army in 1864 during the march from "Atlanta to the Sea."

MOSES CUMMINGS (Autumn, 1903). Nettie took this portrait photograph of her father when he was seventy years old.

Moses returned from the horrors and the hardships of a terrible war to begin life anew on Bird Hill. On August 5, 1866, he married Juliette Barker from Rumford. He later purchased the Abraham Jordan Place and moved the house several hundred feet eastward. His two children by his first marriage continued to live with their aunts, and the couple remained childless for ten years before Juliette gave birth to Nettie, their only child.

Like everyone else on Bird Hill, Moses struggled to wrest a livelihood from the land; by the time this portrait was taken, the Maxim Farm was rapidly expanding. The untimely death of Nettie in 1910, however, was a terrible shock to the couple. It was not long after Nettie was buried in the cemetery down at Locke's Mills that Moses and Juliette left the farm to their son-in-law and moved to Norway to live with Moses' son Eugene and his wife. Despite complaining of ill health most of his life following the Civil War, Moses lived to be ninety-two. He died April 13, 1925, at his son's home.

JULIETTE BARKER CUMMINGS
(November 1903). Nettie took this portrait of
her mother, when Juliette—born October 19,
1839, in Rumford—was about sixty-six years
old. Unfortunately very little information about
Nettie's mother has survived, and she seems
seldom to have posed in Nettie's group
photographs that have been preserved. Juliette
had never been enthusiastic about having a
child and rearing a family; but at age thirty-
nine, she gave birth to Nettie. After Nettie was
born, it became Juliette's intention that her
daughter remain a spinster, live out her life on
the farm, and take care of her and Moses in
their old age. Nettie, of course, lived out her
brief life on the farm, but that life included a
husband and three children. It was a bitter
disappointment to Juliette when Nettie
married. Even more traumatic was her
daughters sudden and unexpected death less
than seven years after this portrait was taken.

MOTHER WITH HAT (1903). Nettie
took this portrait of her mother also in
1903 and very possibly on the same day.
However, in this photograph, Juliette is
sporting a large Victorian floral hat with
veil.

After her daughter's demise, Juliette
and Moses left Bird Hill and the farm to
live in Norway with his son and family.
Juliette died the following year and is
buried in the Cummings' plot in the
cemetery in Locke's Mills.

17

HOWARD MAXIM. Sometime between 1900 and 1910 Nettie had her husband pose in his best suit for this portrait.

Around 1892 or 1893 Moses decided to raise the roof of his farmhouse; and he hired Howard Maxim, a young carpenter from Paris Hill, to assist him in the project. Very likely Juliette was pleased that the house was being enlarged, but certainly she did not anticipate the consequences of her husband hiring the young man from Paris Hill. Her daughter proceeded to fall in love with him, and the two were married on February 17, 1894. It could be said that Juliette "raised the roof" even higher, for she strongly disapproved of the marriage and consequently resented her son-in-law the remainder of her life.

HOWARD MAXIM IN OAT FIELD. Nettie captured her husband standing shoulder high in a field of ripening oats sometime between 1900 and 1909.

Howard did not remain a widower for long. In 1911 he wed Katherine Saunders Chadbourn from Bridgton, born in Nebraska in 1890. The couple went on to rear a large family. However, Howard lost the farm in 1922 on a foreclosure, and he moved his family down from Bird Hill to Locke's Mills where he readily found employment as a machinist at the E.L. Tibbets Spool Company. He seems to have inherited some of the genes of his distant relative, Hiram Stevens Maxim; born in Sangerville, Maine, in 1840, Hiram was the father of over three hundred inventions, including a machine gun. At one time Howard owned stock ($5,000) in the Greenwood Telephone & Telegraph Company and the Bryant's Pond Farmers Union ($10,000).

EARLE MAXIM SAWING WOOD (March 1903). Most children living on farms in rural Maine were held responsible for performing certain daily chores and were expected to work long hours right along with their parents and hired hands during such busy times as haying season and harvest time. Nettie took this photograph of Earle Leslie, her oldest child, assiduously at work sawing stove wood with a bucksaw especially made for him. He was not quite eight years old.

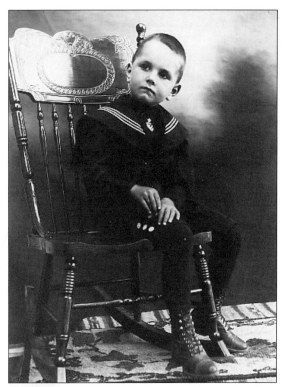

EARLE MAXIM AT FIVE YEARS (1905). Earle Leslie, looking very mature in a sailor blouse, knee pants, and long stockings that were probably held up with garters, sits in a pressed-wood straight-back rocking chair and looks obediently up at his mother's lens. It has been said that Earle abhorred dressing up and posing for his mother's cameras and avoided having his picture taken whenever possible. Since Nettie made most of the family clothes, it is likely that she made his sailor suit. The boots were very likely custom-made by a local shoe and boot maker.

EARLE AND HUNTING DOG (October 12, 1907). Nettie photographed Earle with his rifle over his shoulder, accompanied by his dog, out "gunning" at twelve years of age.

Like his grandfather Moses, he, too, went off to war, but he would never return to Bird Hill. It was his younger brother Walter who received a letter from France written January 28, 1918, with the tragic news that Earle had succumbed to bronchio-pneumonia after first contracting the measles when he joined his regiment a month prior to his death. His regimental commander wrote: "Last night his heart just refused to carry him further." At least Nettie was spared the agony and grief of enduring her first born son's death at the age of twenty-three.

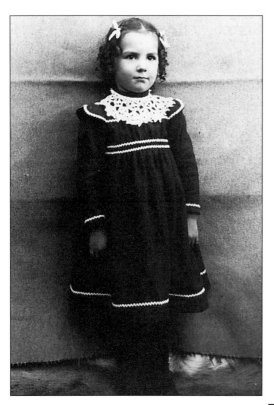

WINNIE MAXIM (Fall 1899) Winnifred Grace, unlike her two brothers, delighted in posing for her mother's cameras. Here, in the fall of 1899, she poses in all her finery in front of a canvas, very likely tacked to the side of the Maxim barn. At three years of age, she has such a happy and vivacious look about her.

The cemeteries throughout rural Maine, including the one on Bird Hill near the Maxim Farm, are mute testimonials that the lives of far too many infants and young children were snatched away from their grieving parents before the age of ten—often victims of a frightful number of dreaded diseases that modern medicine either has eradicated or holds safely in check, such as diphtheria, scarlet fever, and poliomyelitis. Winnie was one of the lucky ones who survived the hazards of childhood and went on to live well beyond her ninety-fifth birthday.

WINNIE AT BEDTIME (November 1902). Nettie photographed her daughter in her long nightgown, her lovely tresses combed down below her shoulders, and holding a candle in her hand as if ready to ascend the stairs—very likely to an unheated bedroom. Since it was November, one can imagine frost-etched designs on the window panes; and perhaps the first late autumn snowfall had covered the sloping frozen fields up there on Bird Hill with a thin layer of snow. The carpet must have felt warm to her bare feet.

The screen that serves as a backdrop in this portrait and others is indicative that Nettie could readily convert one of the rooms in the farmhouse or a platform on the side of the barn into a temporary studio. The light coming from only one direction renders a three-dimensional look to her portraits. Nettie was remarkably adept at the technique of chiaroscuro, focusing just the right amount of light upon the faces of her subjects. In this photograph it is almost as if Winnie were stepping forward out of an indigo night into the silver path of a moonbeam.

WINNIE MAXIM (July 4, 1902). Winnie casts an angelic smile down at her bouquet of roses in this portrait taken when she was six years old. Winnie seems to have been a marvelous little actress who reveled in all the attention from her mother in readying her for this and other portraits. One can just imagine the amount of time Nettie devoted to just curling and embellishing her daughter's hair. Years later Winnie often would relate how fastidious her mother was in preparing and setting up her subjects to photograph. Nettie possibly made the scatter rug on which Winnie is standing, since rug making was another one of her many talents.

WINNIE MAXIM (Spring 1906). Although Winnie was only ten years old when her mother took this portrait in the spring of 1906, her hair style and high neck collar make her appear much older.

By the turn of the century young ladies were no longer encumbered by bustles and several layers of petticoats, although the lace neckpiece Winnie is wearing in a previous photograph and the high neckpiece here could be considered vestiges of her grandmother's day. Large ribbons such as the two Winnie is wearing were popular when Nettie was growing up. This portrait and the others of her children in this collection accent Nettie's creative imagination both in photography and clothing design.

THE LITTLE MOTHER. This photograph of Winnie expressing her motherly instincts was probably taken about the same time as the one above. It is from a postcard in a collection of family memorabilia.

On April 18, 1917, Winnie married Lewis Merrill, who had lived and worked on the Maxim Farm for years. For a while, the newlyweds lived with Winnie's friend and neighbor, Rena and Jack Kimball. After Howard Maxim lost the farm on a foreclosure and he and his second wife moved down to Locke's Mills, Winnie and Lewis rented the farm and would have purchased had they been able to afford it. In 1923 the Merrills left Bird Hill to live in North Bridgton where Lewis worked on the farm of James Chadborn. Winnie had the opportunity to put her motherly instincts to real use in rearing her four children. She died in Bridgton on January 11, 1991.

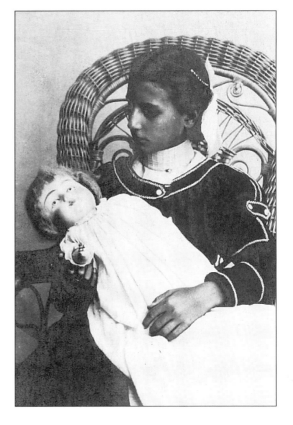

WALTER MAXIM (Summer 1902). Walter was nearly five years old when his mother dressed him up in an outfit very likely worn by his brother Earle two years earlier—including the high ankle shoes—to take this photograph of him obediently sitting on a deerskin rug.

Walter disliked being dressed up and having to pose for his mother's camera nearly as much as his brother Earle did. Therefore, one can speculate that it took some stern persuasion from Nettie to get Walter to flash even this shadow of a smile. Walter and Earle were typical of boys living in rural Maine at that time. They were much more at ease gamboling about in frayed clothing, barefooted from late spring to early autumn. What farm boy felt comfortable so immaculately and formally dressed?

WALTER MAXIM (1902–03). Walter appears to be genuinely happy here in this photograph taken in 1902 or 1903. Even his eyes radiate a smile as he looks slightly upward at the lens. In this portrait, Nettie obviously painstakingly arranged his broad-brimmed straw hat so that the brim would not cast a shadow over his face.

Walter was only nineteen years old when he met and married Etta Hall of Colebrook, New Hampshire, in a double wedding ceremony at the Bird Hill farm with his sister and Lewis Merrill on April 18, 1917. The following January Etta gave birth to Harold Walter in the same room in which Walter had been born on November 16, 1897. In 1920 their daughter Thelma was born, and thirteen months later the couple separated and were divorced.

Walter took his children and went to Florida where he worked as a carpenter for a couple of years. But even though the Maxim Farm was no longer in the family, he felt drawn to Bird Hill. Consequently, in 1925 he returned to his roots and moved into the old Charles Bryant Place where he continued to live for several years after he married Doris Ellingwood in 1928. He died July 9, 1980, on Paris Hill. He was nearly eighty-three.

WALTER, EARLE, AND WINNIE—JACK-O-LANTERNS (1904). It was never an easy task for Nettie to corral all three of her children for a photograph, for the boys usually resisted. But here they seem oblivious to her camera, which is the way she wanted it, as they sit on the split stone granite steps in early autumn, 1904, putting the finishing touches on their Halloween pumpkins.

EARLE, WALTER & WINNIE, PUMPKIN STEM HORNS (1904). Like flute players, Nettie's three children sit on the edge of the corn field and pumpkin patch blowing on pumpkin-stem horns. These were halcyon days for the three siblings. But for Earle and Walter, their lives would change once their father remarried. Earle left the farm to work in Island Pond, Vermont; and at fifteen, Walter ran away to join him.

WINNIE AND WALTER AT THE SPRING (1906). Nettie must have planned well in advance in preparation for taking this jewel of a photograph of Winnie drawing a pail of water with a forked pole from the rustic covered spring at the neighboring Jordan Place, while Walter waits with his tin cup.

The two children, so far removed from any urban center, seem relaxed in their casual home-spun clothes and bare feet. Winnie's sunbonnet is of a style that was commonly worn by country women. One can almost smell the fragrance of wild flowers and hear a soft summer breeze whispering through the tall, unmowed grass.

MOSES CUMMINGS AND WALTER MAXIM (1900). Like a proud old patriarch, Moses Cummings poses for his daughter's camera while sitting in a wicker rocking chair holding his little grandson. Walter, about two-and-a-half years old, seems somewhat stressed having to sit with his stern-looking grandfather.

Three
The Farm

MAXIM FARM. Sometime between 1900 and 1910 Nettie captured this early winter landscape of the Maxim Farm looking down Lower Field to mirror-like North Pond. Very likely it was the thin veil of clouds floating over the still, unfrozen waters of the pond and the interplay of light with the darker and more dominant pewter clouds that attracted her attention on this day. She did, after all, also paint with oils and watercolors, so that here she was using her camera and tripod as she would have used her paintbrush and easel.

THE PLANTING MACHINE (1905). While one man sits on the elevated iron seat holding a tight rein on a sturdy pair of horses, the other man (very likely Howard Maxim) operates the planting machine. Chances are the two were planting corn on this spring day in 1905.

Unlike most hill farms throughout Maine, the Maxim Farm was far from being a postage stamp farm. Over the years acreage was added to the farm until it eventually consisted of around six hundred acres—a large farm by even today's standards here in New England.

For the most part early settlers headed for the high hills to clear the land and build their farms to escape the icy fingers of late spring and early autumn frosts. At least a portion of the Maxim Farm was cleared by Abraham Jordan in 1823, which was quite early, considering Bird Hill lies many miles inland from the coastal area of Maine.

Early farmers such as Abraham Jordan cut down the trees with axes, scooted out the logs with oxen, and burned much of what was left. Again, with the help of their slow-moving oxen, they cleared the land of the huge glacial boulders and built the miles of stonewalls, which remain a testimonial to their Puritan work ethic. They plowed their hardscrabble fields with hand plows pulled by the slow, plodding oxen and later by horses. Land too steep to cultivate went into pasture and hay fields, for one could mow even the steepest fields with scythes.

With the invention of labor-saving machines such as the mowing machine, the reaper, planters (shown above), and manure spreaders, it became increasingly more difficult and less economically feasible to continue working most hill farms, including those on Bird Hill. Rather quickly the hill farms were abandoned. Today, there are none left on Bird Hill, and the many acres of cleared land have been reclaimed by nature. Only the mute stonewalls, old cellar holes marked by clusters of lilacs, a few patches of rhubarb, and an occasional gnarled apple tree are testimonials that Bird Hill was once bristling with farming activities.

UPPER FIELD WITH CORN. Nettie timed this photograph perfectly to catch the lambent sun rays reflecting off the dark green leaves of the corn stocks while at the same time capturing this spectacular panorama of Lower Field and North Pond with its three tiny islands surrounded by undulating hills. There is fine depth to this photograph.

These well-manicured sloping fields, so smooth and boulder free, exemplify the extent to which generations of Maine farmers were bonded to the land and the pride they took in carving productive farms out of the forest-covered glacial hills such as Bird Hill. Nettie Maxim and her cameras have provided visual evidence of their Herculean efforts.

THE CORN HARVEST. Nettie returned to Upper Field in early fall with her camera to photographs these shocks of corn neatly stacked like Indian wigwams to dry. One can almost hear the rustling of the autumn wind ascending Bird Hill. Only a small patch of corn remains standing, waiting for the harvesters of corn to return with their sickles. The shocks and pumpkins will be gathered up in a horse-drawn wagon and conveyed to the barn to feed the livestock. After the remaining small patch of corn has been cut, only the stubble will remain to be turned under by a steel-mold board plow. Such is the cycle of life.

WORKING THE FIELD. Sometime in the first decade after the turn of the century Nettie photographed this farmer, probably her husband, dressed in foul weather gear as if headed out on the windswept sea to fish for cod. But instead, he is holding a long set of reins—guiding his horse and spraying machine carefully between the rows of a sea of potatoes. Every farm family in Maine raised at least enough potatoes to keep themselves well supplied from one season to the other and enough for seed to plant in the spring. Many Maine farms, like the Maxim Farm, raised potatoes to ship to the city markets. Maine farmers had to be diversified in order to survive.

POTATOES IN BLOOM. This healthy weed-free field of potatoes in full blossom, resembling crested waves sweeping across a broad expanse of ocean, presages a bountiful harvest in September. From the size of this field, it is very likely that Howard Maxim and his father-in-law, Moses Cummings, used a horse-drawn potato harvester. Howard, who very early in life had evinced a proclivity for machines, possessed not only the ability to maintain and repair his own machinery, but also to invent all sorts of labor-saving devices.

HOWARD IN THE POTATO FIELD. Only a photographer such as Nettie—who was born, reared, and lived out her life on a farm—could possibly have the appreciation of the subtle day-to-day and even hourly changes that occur and how transitory the beauty of nature can be on a New England farm. A potato field does not remain in full blossom for very long. A sudden gust of wind and the blossoms are air borne, leaving the plants bereft of their floral pulchritude.

If Nettie looked at a potato field through the eyes of an aesthete, Howard viewed his fields largely through the eyes of a pragmatist. The slightest oversight or failure to check one's crops almost daily can be disastrous. Farmer or photographer, one must be circumspect.

THE POTATO HARVEST. Rows of dug potatoes, like miniatures of the glacial boulders once cleared from this lower Maxim field to build the stonewall separating field from pasture, lie in long furrows to dry briefly in the sun before being gathered in sacks and barrels. Most of this bountiful harvest photographed by Nettie in early September of 1905, would have been graded, packed, and hauled down the hill in wagons to the railroad station at Locke's Mills to be shipped to Portland and beyond.

The two men standing back to back in the distance are digging the potatoes by hand, taking care not to pierce any of the potatoes with the prongs.

FRAMING THE BARN (1902). The Maxim children—Walter, Earle, and Winnie—look on with great interest as their father sits astride a tongued beam, drilling a hole with a mortise auger, one winter day in 1902 when all of Bird Hill was covered with unsullied snow.

In the 1899 Maine State Board of Agriculture Bulletin titled "Barn Construction," Howard wrote a paragraph indicating his plans to build a new and more efficient barn "as soon as we can save the money to pay for it . . . When I build I intend to build with basement and build large enough to house all stock, and the larger part of the wagons and tools under one roof."

A common plan for a post-and-beam barn constructed before and after the turn of the century was to have a central driving and feeding floor with a tie-up for cattle on one side (preferably the south side) and a ground mow on the other. Additional hay lofts would be located on the second and perhaps even a third level, depending upon the height of the barn. Hay usually was raised and stored in the upper lofts, loose of course, either by passing each forkful from level to level or by a hayfork and pulley with a long rope. The rope would be attached to a whiffletree and traces hooked to a horse. When the horse was driven forward, the huge forkfuls of hay would be hoisted to the upper lofts. There was also space on the opposite side of the driving and feeding floor from the tie-up for the storage of carriages, wagons, and machinery. There would also be space on this side for horse stalls. The barn itself was usually built on a solid foundation of split granite stones with a basement partly or totally above ground. The manure was kept directly under the tie-up and also under the horse stalls where the pigs were usually kept and allowed to root. The manure would be taken out in the spring and spread on the fields and plowed land as soon as the snow had melted and the surface was sufficiently dry and firm. A portion of the basement was also usually reserved for the storage of wagons and machines.

34

BARN RAISING (1902). What really sets Nettie Maxim apart from other published Maine photographers is that she lived all of her life on a hill farm and could readily record with her cameras the broad spectrum of activities which took place on a farm from one season to another and such major events as barn raising. The building of the Maxim barn may very well have been the only one she ever witnessed. Perhaps she did not realize at the time that she would be making a valuable contribution to Americana with these two excellent photographs of her own husband constructing a typical post-and-beam barn in 1902.

This photograph in particular is an excellent testimonial to Howard's ingenuity. It is said that he built the entire barn with only the aid of a well-trained and obedient horse. With a pulley and rope, including one running down to the ground where it was attached to a whiffletree and traces hooked to his horse, he was able to raise each heavy beam (such as the one to which the pulley is attached). He simply gave a verbal signal and the horse would slowly begin to move forward just as it would when raising a forkful of hay into the lofts. Simultaneously Howard would begin doing what he is seen doing in this photograph—pulling the rope running through the pulley. What is so remarkable is that craftsmen such as Howard, using primitive tools by today's standards, constructed such imposing and enduring framework without nails and spikes. All the beams and poles were fitted together by the mortise and tenon method, and sturdy wooden pegs were used instead of spikes.

Little did Howard or Nettie perceive that within twenty years after this prodigious undertaking was completed, the farm would be lost. It is a sad moment for any farmer to see his livestock driven out of the barn for the last time and hauled away. All that remains today is the moss-covered stone foundation and a few badly decomposed beams.

JERSEY COWS (1902). A fine trio of thoroughbred Jerseys crop the grass in this hardscrabble pasture on the Maxim Farm. Jerseys were more popular at the turn of the century because of the high butterfat content in their milk. In Nettie's day almost every rural family kept one or more cows to provide them with milk, butter, and cream.

APPLE PICKING (1906–07). Harvesting apples was a family activity on the Maxim Farm. Howard (on the ladder), Moses, Earle (on the stepladder), and Winnie are picking, while Walter is being careful not to bruise any of the apples as he pours them from his picking basket into a larger basket. Nettie very likely heaped the barrels high with apples for this photograph.

FATHER LINING BEES (July 1902). The old Civil War veteran was photographed in 1903 holding a fir branch with a swarm of wild bees he located and captured to add to his bee hives. Beekeeping and apple growing were and are symbiotic. The bees pollinate the trees and gather the nectar from the blossoms to produce large quantities of honey for domestic use and to market.

HOWARD MAXIM AND CHICKS (June 1908). A large flock of two or three-week-old chicks have adopted Howard as he attempts to work over a pile of sifted loam on a June day in 1908. By the size of this flock, Howard must either have hatched these chickens with a kerosene-burning incubator or purchased them from a hatchery. Almost every rural family kept a small flock of laying hens.

WINNIE MAXIM AND BANTAMS (1904). Bantams were popular pets for children living in rural areas. Nettie took this photograph of her daughter with a bantam hen and her little brood of month-old chicks sometime in late spring, 1904.

HOWARD FEEDING LAMBS (Spring 1906). On an ebullient spring day in 1906, Nettie captured her husband kneeling in the pasture feeding a trio of lambs, probably born in February. To the left a ewe stands under an old apple tree with two spring-born lambs. As versatile as Nettie was, it is very possible that she saved a fleece or two each year to spin into yarn to make rugs and clothing.

HOWARD FEEDING TWO LAMBS. Howard seems to be enjoying himself as he holds two winter-born lambs and a pan of grain, while the mother ewe contentedly grazes behind him. The Maxim Farm was a typical general farm in Maine around the turn of the century in that the farm supplied the extended family with most of what it needed and a wide variety of produce to market—such as livestock, milk, butter, wool, eggs, honey, apples, small fruit, and vegetables— cash income. In the winter most farmers logged and cut cordwood.

FAMILY AND FARMHANDS (1908). The Maxim Farm was a beehive of activity in the summer of 1908 when Nettie took this photograph of her family and hired help posing on the porch and steps of the farmhouse. From left to right are: (front row) unknown, Walter, Earle, and Winnie; (second row) unknown, James Chadbourne, Vernon Curtis, and unknown; (third row) Jennie Bradbury, unknown, Lura Bradbury, and unknown; (back row) Howard Maxim (with Bess the cat on his shoulder), Henrietta Saunders, Herb Day?, and Mary Bradbury.

THE GROVE AND MOUNT ABRAM (1903–04). Bird Hill and its surroundings, including Mount Abram in the distance, were slowly emerging from the long winter hiatus in the spring of either 1903 or 1904 when Nettie took this photograph of the grove of young birches not far from the house. Early spring was an auspicious time of year for everyone on Bird Hill.

ELIAS AND THE RAVEN. Could Nettie possibly have been alluding to Edgar Allen Poe's immortal poem *The Raven* when she gave the romantic title—"Elias and the Raven"—to this photograph (taken sometime between 1900 and 1910) of Elias Bartlett and the pigeon perched on top of his head?

Elias Bartlett was a hired hand at the Maxim Farm, who came from East Bethel. He was a simple soul toward whom Howard made a special effort to be paternalistic. He made every endeavor to prevent the other farmhands and his own children from ridiculing Elias. For some inexplicable reason the pigeon adopted Elias and followed him around the farm, frequently perching on his head and shoulders.

EDGAR GROVER, SON OF WILL (1909). Nettie's mastery of the art of portrait photography is exemplified in this photograph and the one below of Edgar, the son of Will Grover—a hired man on the Maxim Farm. Nettie took this photograph of little Edgar, flashing a smile as scintillating as the floriferous day in May 1909, sitting happily in a wicker baby carriage beneath a canopy of apple blossoms.

EDGAR GROVER (1909). Nettie, either before or after the above photograph, substituted the family wicker rocking chair for the wicker baby carriage in this portrait taken inside the Maxim house, with the help of the sunlight from the window to the left.

BIRCHES. Not even multi-layers of deep snow kept Nettie and her camera indoors. A sun-filled morning after an ice storm that had transformed Bird Hill into a dazzling world of crystal provided this magnificent setting that fired Nettie's aesthetic imagination to a white heat. Here she focused on these two graceful twin birches, their branches like crystal chandeliers. Her timing was perfect, for at any moment a gust of wind could sweep down from the distant hills to send the incandescent ice shattering into a million pieces over the thin layer of pearlescent crust.

WINNIE FEEDING LAMB (June 4, 1904). Nettie captured her daughter at the age of eight playing the role of little mother to this cosset lamb her grandfather had given her for her birthday. Obviously the mother ewe had refused to nurse the lamb, perhaps because she had given birth to twins or possibly even triplets. At any length, Winnie must have been kept busy for many weeks until her lamb could be weaned from this interesting bottle converted into a nursing bottle. She must have taken great delight in having this lamb, not more than two weeks old, gambol about with her wherever she went either on the farm or to visit playmates on neighboring farms.

Four
Berry Picking

PICKING #3 FIELD (1905). What really set the Maxim Farm apart from the other farms on Bird Hill is that Moses and Howard, in addition to running a general farm, developed a specialty which, over the years, became a major operation and the principal source of revenue for the family. They cultivated upwards to 17 acres of raspberries and blackberries and shipped them by rail from Locke's Mills to Portland and beyond.

Nettie, of course, was active with her camera during the berry harvest. She photographed this healthy field of raspberries, so high that one can barely see the heads of some of the taller pickers.

BERRY CREW AND TEAM (1909). This is no mid-summer outing. During the peak of the berry-picking season, fifty or more pickers were hired to harvest literally tons of raspberries and blackberries that ripened on the carefully tended bushes.

Each morning Will Grover, who was employed to work on the farm the year-round, would hitch up the team of horses to the farm wagon loaded with crates of berries picked the previous day, and trundle down the rutted road a mile or so to the railroad station at Locke's Mills, from which the berries would be shipped to Portland via the Grand Trunk Railroad. A major buyer in Portland was Cummings Brothers, who were related to Moses Cummings. Hay's Drug Store in Portland, makers of Hay's Five Fruit—a soda fountain syrup blended from the natural juices of five fruits—purchased berries from the Maxim Farm.

After the berries had been unloaded at the station, local pickers who did not board at the farm on Bird Hill would be conveyed up to the farm to take part in the daily harvest.

Sitting in his father's lap looking directly into Nettie's lens is one of her favorite subjects, little tow-headed Edgar Grover. Nettie obviously delayed the picking operation this morning to arrange the crew for maximum effect. Will Grover is driving the team of horses, Spot and Dan. Among the crew members who can be identified are Earle Maxim, Lyman Herrick, Winnie Hadagin, Fred Spear, Wnora Spear, Georgia Marion Swift, Ruth Farrington, Alice Cross, and Mary Elizabeth Swift.

46

PICKING #2 FIELD (1905). In this photograph Nettie was able to illustrate the magnitude of the berry-picking operation on the farm. Here the extensive #2 field, with a patchwork backdrop of farms and higher hills beyond, is mottled with pickers of all ages with their picturesque Edwardian hats. Obviously, for a couple of months in the summer the Maxim Farm provided employment for a large number of local people.

BERRY FIELD (1902–03). This is a fine closeup of little Winnie, wearing a single braid, carrying a basket containing 4 quarts of raspberries. To her left is Charles Vetquosky, a young Polish immigrant.

JENNY BRADBURY (1908). With the eye of a portrait painter, Nettie singled out Jenny Bradbury from the host of women berry pickers to pose for her camera in the summer of 1908. Indeed, it is a striking pose with the brim of her straw hat turned up, probably at Nettie's suggestion so not to cast a shadow over her face. Although Jenny might not be considered beautiful, there is a look of strength and character in her finely-chiseled facial features.

MAXIM BERRY PICKERS (1905). Earl Farrington, the field boss—dressed more as if he were going on a Sunday picnic—surveys the berry-picking operation during the summer of 1905. In fact, most of the pickers seem rather impeccably and picturesquely dressed as they mingle among the endless rows of berry bushes. Contrary to her two brothers, Winnie, standing in front to the far right, seldom missed an opportunity to be in a photograph. North Pond is in the distance.

BERRY PICKERS DAY OFF (1905). On their day off these berry pickers have caught enough fish for a fish fry for the entire Maxim berry crew.

CHASE PLACE. The old Chase Place was rather a typical Maine farm built in the first half of the nineteenth century with the house, ell, shed, and barn all attached. Around 1845 Richard Jordan purchased the property from John B. Knight, an early Bird Hill settler, and constructed these buildings. As William Berry Lapham, the local historian and former Bird Hill resident, wrote in the June 9, 1885, issue of the Oxford *Democrat*: "He built good buildings." Jordan eventually sold the property to John Chase from Paris, Maine.

CHASE PLACE WITH APPLE BLOSSOMS. Nettie captured the very essence of a rural Maine hill farm in late spring. The Chase house peeks around the veil of apple blossoms and down at the rutted Bird Hill road.

BOARDING HOUSE GROUP (1905). By 1905 the berry aspect of the farm had expanded to the extent that Howard purchased the Chase Place to house many of his pickers. Part of the 1905 crew, including Annie and Ed Carpenter, are sitting in front of their boarding house.

BERRY PICKERS, MAXIM FARM (1907). The 1907 crew is photographed on the steps of the Chase Place. From left to right are: (front row) Winnie Maxim, Margaret Herrick, Frances Cummings, Beatrice Stevens, Jenny Bradbury, Walter Maxim, Grace Stevens, and Ida Morgan; (middle row) Hattie Jenny, Veda Jenny, Mrs. Hammond, Mrs. Bradbury (cook), Ora Field, and Lura Bradbury; (back row) George Everett, Arthur Herrick, Charles Mason, Ida Aldrich, Fred Mason, Ethel Ellingwood, Ethel Woodis, Florence Cummings, Lucy Emmons, and Elson Hammond.

ROMANCE IN THE BERRY FIELDS. Nettie staged this touching romantic scene of Lura Bradbury and James Chadbourne—the tray boy—sometime between 1905 and 1909, embracing behind a row of raspberries.

Little did anyone, least of all Nettie, anticipate the tragic event that lay ahead. In 1910 James, who stayed at the Maxim Farm, was stricken with diphtheria after returning from Berlin, New Hampshire. Nettie nursed him back to health but in turn contracted the dreaded disease, and all of Bird Hill and its surroundings were shocked when she succumbed to the illness on May 29, 1910. Her promising career as a photographer had barely begun. She was buried in the cemetery at Locke's Mills in the town of Greenwood.

Five

Gene's Family

GENE CUMMINGS FAMILY (August 1906). Nettie's half brother Gene, his wife Inez, and their two daughters—Florence to the left and Frances to the right—were relaxing in the shade of the woodbine at his father's farm on Bird Hill when Nettie took this family photograph in August 1906. Gene and his family were favorite subjects for Nettie and her camera. This whimsical pose indicates that they were also cooperative subjects.

GENE CUMMINGS (June 1902).
Gene, who was born Eli Eugene on Bird
Hill to Moses and his first wife (Julia)
on September 12, 1858, was a
handsome gentleman in his forties when
Nettie took this fine portrait of him in
June 1902 with her 5-by-7-inch format
camera. She had wasted little time in
honing her skills as a photographer.

INEZ BEAN CUMMINGS (June 1902).
Since this portrait of Gene's wife was
also taken in June 1902, it is very likely
that Nettie took both portraits on the
same day. The fact that she used only
one flash powder tray to supplement the
natural light is very evident here.

Inez was the daughter of Benjamin W.
Bean and Sarah Swett Bean and the
sister of Leon Leonwood Bean, better
known as L.L. Bean. She died in 1919 at
the age of fifty-one.

FLORENCE CUMMINGS (1906).
Nettie took this portrait of her niece
dressed up as a berry picker at the Maxim
Farm. Florence was nearly fifteen. Her
features and light-colored clothing stand
out well against the dark backdrop of an
apple tree laden with fruit.

Later in life Florence often said that
she did not like to have her aunt take her
photograph because, as she said, "I wasn't
as pretty as my sister."

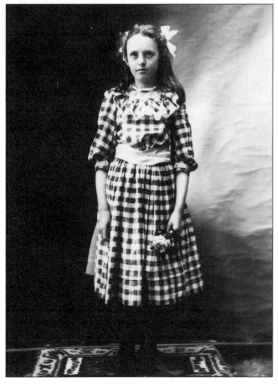

FRANCES CUMMINGS (1903).
Indeed, Frances was a pretty girl with
her long tresses and a large white
ribbon, looking slightly upwards into
her aunt's lens. She was ten years old
when Nettie took this portrait of her
niece holding a rose and standing on a
scatter rug.

GENE'S HOUSE (August 1908). Nettie took this photograph of Gene's house, located at 23 Paris Street in Norway. It was to this house with Gene's family that Moses and Juliette moved shortly after Nettie's tragic death. Juliette died here soon after their arrival, but Moses continued to live here until his own death on April 23, 1925. Despite complaining of ill health most of his life, the old Civil War veteran lived several months beyond his ninety-second birthday. He, too, is buried in the family plot at the cemetery in Locke's Mills, Greenwood, just a mile or so down the hill from the farm he loved so dearly.

GENE'S FAMILY (c. 1902). Presumably Nettie took this portrait of her brother Gene Inez and his family at the farm on Bird Hill. Gene is holding his older daughter Florence, while Frances stands behind her parents. The boards on the side of the barn are visible around the edges of Nettie's canvas backdrop.

FLORENCE AND FRANCES (1902). Sometime in the summer of 1902 Nettie captured this precious moment in the lives of Florence and Frances when she photographed her two young nieces playing with their dolls up at the farm. The dolls certainly would be wonderful collector's items today.

FLORENCE AND FRANCES
(c. 1906). Dressed for berry picking, Florence and Frances pose for Nettie's camera in front of a screen tacked to the side of the barn on Bird Hill. Both girls were in their teens when this photograph was taken around 1906.

Florence eventually married Walter Bailey, and the couple lived most of their lives in Andover where they reared a family. Frances remained in her hometown of Norway where she married Howard Lasselle and also reared a family.

TENTING OUT (1904). Sometime in the summer of 1904 Gene and his family posed for this photograph in front of their tent during an outing on Bird Hill.

AN OUTING ON SOUTH POND (August 1906). It would be difficult to imagine Howard being able to spare the time from the farm for a leisurely family outing; but somehow Nettie, despite the great demands made upon her, managed to join Gene and his family on a number of outings such as the one here at South Pond. Here she photographed Gene pushing a rowboat off Littlefield's Beach and about to jump into the bow while Frances is preparing to row. Florence is facing her sister while Inez sits in the stern with a fishing rod beside her.

FLORENCE CUMMINGS (Spring 1906). Even though Florence was self-conscious about what she considered her lack of prettiness, Nettie managed to photograph her on a number of occasions. Here she appears to be totally absorbed in a book. The more urbane and genteel lifestyle of Gene's family is a marked contrast to that of the Maxims up on Bird Hill. Yet, it would appear that Nettie, having briefly been a teacher, understood and appreciated both worlds.

THE MUSIC HOUR (c. 1902). Inez is playing the organ while Frances practices the violin in this fine interior photograph Nettie took around 1902. Parlor organs were popular musical instruments in rural Maine homes.

NEWSBOY, NORWAY (1904). The little newsboy collecting "his" money from Inez for the *Lewiston Journal* in this superb photograph taken in Norway in 1904 is in reality Frances, whom her aunt dressed up to look like a newsboy.

Perhaps this photograph more than any other that Nettie took of Gene and his family evinces the affection Nettie harbored for him, his wife, and their two daughters, and how comfortable she was interacting with them in a world quite different from the one up on Bird Hill.

Six
Bird Hill

VIEW FROM BIRD HILL. From Charles Jordan's field near the Bird Hill schoolhouse, Nettie captured this broad panorama, including North Pond. The smooth, sloping, and carefully manicured field epitomizes the pride which Maine farmers at the turn of the century took in maintaining their farms. As with all the other long-abandoned fields on Bird Hill and elsewhere throughout rural Maine, the trees have marched back and reclaimed what was once theirs.

Bird Hill was initially called Berry Hill after Levi Berry, the hill's first settler. The name was changed after the Berrys moved off the hill and three sons of John Bird of Norway purchased farms from the Berrys and John Lapham.

ABE BRYANT AND OXEN (1906). Both the sturdy yoke of oxen and Abe Bryant, posing in 1906 for Nettie's camera, are symbolic of rural Maine before and after the turn of the century. Together they cleared the land of trees and boulders and smoothed and tilled the glacial soil.

There were about ten families scattered over Bird Hill by the turn of the century. The Birds, like their predecessors the Berrys, had vacated the hill that bore their name, and their farms were taken over by newcomers. And with the arrival of the Vetquosky family, a new ethnic group was added to this rather remote rural microcosm.

Fortunately, through the writings of Dr. William Berry Lapham, grandson of Levi Berry, the original families who first began clearing and farming the land in this isolated section of the town of Bethel bordering both the towns of Greenwood and Woodstock are known. He memorialized the first fifty years of the history of Bird Hill and the people who were a part of this history in an article he wrote for the Oxford *Democrat* on June 9, 1885.

In Nettie's generation, most of the old farms that had survived had been expanded; and Bird Hill had about reached its zenith in terms of agriculture and the amount of cleared acreage. Ineluctably, however, Bird Hill was destined to go the way of many rural areas—especially the hill farms—during the first half of the twentieth century. Today, only the Ransom Cummings farmhouse and shed have survived the vagaries of time. All the other farms, constructed with such skill, and the surrounding fields, once tended with such loving care, have vanished. If it were not for Nettie Maxim and her splendid photography, the only visual evidence that several generations once tamed this land through hard work and perseverance would be a tiny cemetery and the miles of mute stonewalls, hidden cellar holes, and rusty broken plow shares.

PROCTOR'S PLACE (August 8, 1908). Nettie saw the aesthetic beauty in the vintage farms on Bird Hill. The Frank Proctor (Charles Bryant) Place was a classical New England set of farm buildings with the weathered clapboard house and ell, serving mainly as a woodshed and sheltered passageway to the barn. The sidelights on each side of the front door, which very likely was seldom if ever used, indicates that the house was probably built before 1850. In the spring of 1919, Nettie's son Walter purchased this farm with 30 acres for $500. He lived here with his first wife and two children until 1923.

ABE BRYANT AND TEAM (1906). Abe Bryant proudly stands with his ox team while Earle, Winnie, and Walter pose in the ox cart for their mother.

THE CHASE PLACE (1905–10). Bird Hill is locked in the early throes of winter in this Nettie Maxim scene of New Road winding north by the forsaken old Chase Place.

LAST CLASS AT BIRD HILL SCHOOL (1903). Nettie truly chronicled in the winter of 1903 a very precious moment in time with this photograph of the very last class ever to be held on Bird Hill. Earle, Walter, Winnie, Grover Thomas, and Alice Buck pose with their teacher, Alma Swan, at the entrance of the old Chase Place, which for one year served as a school, the original little one-room red school house having been abandoned earlier.

Henceforth, the children were conveyed to and from Locke's Mills in a wagon or sled drawn by a team of horses. Once the road down the hill was solidly packed, the boys preferred sliding down to Locke's Mills on their double runner sleds, made with two sleds attached to a wide plank, often big enough to hold six boys. On an icy road, according to one of the boys, the last mile could be covered in a little over a minute, but it took real skill to negotiate the last sharp turn.

LEDGE, BIRD HILL ROAD. Nettie photographed the narrow, sinuous road leading to the top of Bird Hill in every season, but she seems to have been particularly intrigued by the natural beauty of this megalithic outcropping still referred to as the "Ledge." At the turn of the century, most country roads were packed down by snowrollers pulled by two to three pairs of horses, or sometimes oxen. But the Bird Hill Road was broken open after each storm by an older method—chaining a log cross-wise under the front runners of a logging sled or bobsled and with one or more teams of horses, dragging the road. Frank Vetquosky kept this road open for many years.

MID-MOUNTAIN FARM. This attractive set of farm buildings, including the well-maintained Greek Revival house, with an extra long ell—a portion of which apparently served as a summer kitchen—was built by Abraham Bryant. Later it was passed on to his son Benjamin and then to Josiah George, and eventually to his daughter Serena (Rena) and her husband, Jack Kimball.

Before the popularity of the automobile, the Maine hills attracted many summer visitors who came to breathe the clear air and to savor good country cooking. Mid-Mountain Farm, like many other farms in rural Maine, took in summer borders.

MT. ABRAM FROM MID-MOUNTAIN FARM. Mt. Abram looms above the serrated conifers and the covered fields at Mid-Mountain Farm.

66

RENA GEORGE WITH FAN (1905).
Nettie added a touch of the mystique to
her rural photography and Bird Hill
when in 1905 she had her friend Rena
George pose in this immaculately white
Edwardian dress—veiling a portion of her
face with a fan like a Spanish "condesa."

This particular photograph is a
valuable addition to the Nettie Maxim
collection, because it represents one of
the few times she apparently attempted
to take an outdoor photograph at night.

RENA GEORGE (1905). This
photograph of Rena was very likely taken
on the same occasion as the above
photograph—her graduation from Gould
Academy. However, this photograph was
taken outdoors in the daylight without
the use of flash powder. As she so often
did with outside portraits, she tacked a
screen on the side of the barn. Without
the fan, one has an excellent view of
Rena's exquisitely delicate lace neck
piece.

CELIA ESTES (1902). Nettie captured her niece, Celia May Estes, exuding unsophisticated charm and dressed as a country woman might have dressed even before the nineteenth century.

Celia was Moses' granddaughter from his first marriage to Julia Cushman Cummings, who died while he was fighting in the Civil War. Celia was the daughter of Benjamin Franklin Estes and Emma Cummings, who had been adopted after Julia's death by Jacob and Parazina Chase. Although Celia appears to be wearing a wedding band, it was not until 1911 when she was twenty-seven that she married William Warren Chadbourne of North Bridgton. The couple had two children.

CELIA ESTES FEEDING LAMB (May 1900). Celia, who was fifteen years old when her aunt took this photograph of her feeding grain to a weaned lamb, was a favorite photographic subject for Nettie and a friend of Rena George. Her mother Emma, Nettie's half sister, had died December 29, 1888, at the age of twenty-seven. Celia spent much of her childhood on the Bird Hill farm of her grandfather Moses and her aunt Nettie.

CELIA ESTES READING (June 1904). In marked contrast to the two previous photographs, Celia posed in June 1904, dressed as a more sophisticated and genteel lady in an almost classical reclining position while reading a book. This seems to have been a popular pose for informal portraits at the turn of the century. Presumably Nettie took this indoor photograph at the farm on Bird Hill, for Celia is said to have spent much of her time on Bird Hill after her mother's demise. It is very likely Nettie made the pillow on which Celia is resting her book.

CELIA ESTES AND RENA GEORGE (June 1904). Only a few of Nettie's photographs appear to have been spontaneous. The early cameras were cumbersome and staging scenes to photograph was essential. Nettie is known to have scouted a year or so in advance for potential sites for good photographs. This lovely scene taken in June 1904, of Celia and Rena, two dear friends, is a paragon of Nettie's attention to detail, composition, and aesthetics.

UNCLE RANSOM'S PLACE (May 1, 1904). Of the eleven farms on Bird Hill in Nettie's day, only her Uncle Ransom's farmhouse, originally known as the Eli Cushman Place, has survived the years to remind us that Bird Hill was once a thriving agricultural community. All of the others, like their previous owners, have vanished from the hill. Modern, and very likely less enduring, houses have recently sprung up in sections of the long abandoned land.

CUMMINGS GROUP (1903–04). Occasionally the Maxims and Cummings were able to spare time for an outing. From left to right are Roscoe Cummings, Walter Maxim, Moses Cummings, Earle Maxim, unknown, Mamie Beal, Lena Cummings, Howard Maxim, and Winnie Maxim. Predictably, Nettie's mother is absent from the photograph.

RANSOM CUMMINGS. Uncle Ransom, who never fought in war, poses for his niece's camera with a Civil War musket, bayonet, and powder horn. Ransom, born in 1837, was the son of Joseph Cummings and Cinderilla Lapham Cummings, and was the brother of Moses. It was on his farm, the former Eli Cushman Place, that Moses' first wife—Julia—was born.

ELMER CUMMINGS. The dandified son of Uncle Roscoe, Moses' other brother, poses for his cousin with a Winchester lever-action hunting rifle. This photograph was probably taken at Nettie's platform out beside the barn with a painted screen in the background and something made to look like snow on the carpet under his feet. Elmer hardly seems attired for the occasion and the late spring scene on the canvas backdrop also seems incongruent. This was unusual for Nettie's photography.

VIEW FROM THE CHARLES JORDAN FARM (1905). Bird Hill lies deep beneath several layers of snow in this photograph Nettie took in 1905. Maine winters were long and taxing on humans and beasts at the turn of the century. The women on many of the more isolated farms, such as Uncle Ransom's (visible in the distance), were virtually imprisoned from the first snowfall until the end of mud season. Bird Hill, nearly void of trees in 1905, mirrors the extent to which early Maine hill farms were cleared for hay, pasturage, and crops.

JORDAN PLACE (c. 1905). The Jordan Place, first owned by Richard Jordan, the father of Charles Jordan, was a simple Cape attached directly to a weathered barn and cow shed.

BIRD HILL GROUP (1907). Some of the younger Bird Hill set pose seated on the split stone steps at the Maxim Farm for Nettie in the summer of 1907. From left to right are Charles Vetquosky, Celia Estes, Bill Perham, Serena George, and Francis Vetquosky.

LEDGE, BIRD HILL ROAD. The narrow road passing by the Ledge and leading up to Bird Hill was obviously one of Nettie's favorite spots along the road. The road through here still remains unpaved and nearly as narrow; but with extensive land development now taking place on Bird Hill, this quaint country road seems destined to be altered.

THE LOVE LETTER (1904). Nettie was obviously a wonderful romantic, who took advantage of every opportunity to stage a romantic scene at some carefully selected site that provided an effective stage setting or backdrop for her contrived dramatic episodes. Once again she chose Celia Estes, a favorite subject, who seemed readily available and willing to cooperate with her aunt and her fertile imagination.

For "The Love Letter," Nettie also chose one of her choice spots on the Bird Hill Road. The old rustic fence opposite the Ledge provided a perfect backdrop for Celia to pose, reading a letter from a real or imaginary lover. It was the summer of 1904. She was nineteen.

THE LOVE LETTER (1904). And now, letter folded in her hand, Celia evinces an aura of beatitude.

Like most artists, Nettie's personality seems to be reflected in her photography. Bird Hill appeared to be so meaningful for her; and if there were moments of sadness and despair, she kept those moments out of the lenses of her camera. The real tragedies that might have altered her personality in some way—the death of Earle and the loss of the farm—came after her demise, which in one sense, tempers the tragedy of her early death.

Both of these photographs are measuring sticks of Nettie's skill as a photographer and her ability to take full advantage of any natural light. Despite the amount of shade and Celia's dark dress and hat, Nettie utilized very effectively the limited amount of sunlight filtering through the heavy foliage so that Celia is not swallowed up by her surroundings.

SUMMER ROMANCE (1905–07). As on several other occasions, Arthur Herrick, who worked summers during berry-picking season as a tray boy, and Frances Cummings pose as teenage lovers. Here they sit holding hands in a hammock at the Chase Place. The undulating crossroads is a marvelous setting for two young lovers planning their future, but each was destined to take a a different road. Arthur would marry Eva Glines and live in Bethel where they reared two daughters. He would become a machinist and own his own garage. Frances would marry Howard Lasselle of Norway in 1912 and also have two children.

THE CAST (1909). Probably one of Nettie's last photographs was of this young group in a local play performed at Mt. Abram Hotel, Locke's Mills. From left to right are: (front row) Dana Grant Jr., Ruth Farrington, and Carol Cushman; (back row) Ruth Stowell, James Chadbourne, Lorna Littlehale, ? Tompson (mill boss), Vernon Curtis, Serena George, and Earle Maxim.

ROAD TO LOCKE'S MILLS (January 1907). The long, rigorous winters seem not to have dulled Nettie's aesthetic eye for the wondrous transformation of Bird Hill after a winter storm. On this January day she was out with her camera somewhere on the road to Locke's Mills. The temperature apparently moderated during a snowfall. Although candescent snow clings to the bows of the conifers, the skeletal branches of the deciduous trees are coated with silvery ice and perhaps a touch of hoary frost.

One can almost hear the jingling of sleigh bells or the more rhythmic clanging of a bell or two on a passing horse-drawn bobsled, loaded with logs destined for the insatiable sawmill down in the village, or perhaps with next winter's cordwood to keep the home fires burning and beat back the frost on sub-zero nights that often sent iron nails rocketing into the frigid blackness of night.

BIRD HILL ROAD (1906). "Whose woods these are I think I know. His house is in the village, though; He will not see me stopping here To watch his woods fill up with snow."

Nettie died thirteen years before Robert Frost wrote this lovely first stanza of the poem titled *Stopping by Woods on a Snowy Evening*, but in several ways they were kindred spirits—she capturing with her camera the imagery that Frost succeeded in conveying with his pen.

One could be envious of Nettie and the person sitting quietly in the sleigh, absorbing an exquisitely enchanting world in the aftermath of a gentle snowfall. The pace of life then moved no faster than the horse and even the methodical ox. The few who did own automobiles stored them in the barns and sheds with the first snowfall and only began driving them again after mud season.

JULIA McCONNELL AND DAUGHTER (1901–02). Julia McConnell, a neighbor on Bird Hill, poses with her tiny daughter Elvia in this portrait, probably taken out by the Maxim barn. Julia's elaborate floral hat is an example of the creativity of the milliners at the turn of the century.

LEDGE, BIRD HILL ROAD. By now this has become a familiar site. For those traveling the still meandering, narrow dirt road leading up to a very different Bird Hill from the one Nettie Maxim knew so intimately and photographed in such detail, this spot is still identifiable. The rustic fence has long since vanished, but the "Ledge" remains—a reminder that nature's creativity is much more likely to endure than that of humankind.

This time, however, Nettie is traveling down the Bird Hill Road to Locke's Mills and perhaps slightly beyond. But her world and her photography were centered on Bird Hill.

Seven
Summertime

NORTH POND AND BOAT. Sometime during her brief but productive career as a photographer Nettie took this photograph of placid North Pond and this square-stern rowboat tied to the pond's sylvan shore.

    At the turn of the century there were few cottages built along the shores of even the largest lakes in Maine, like Moosehead and Sebago, and certainly there were no motor boats to muffle the cry of loons, the melodic songs of warblers, or even the raucous cawing of a crow from the tip of a tall pine. Except for an occasional sandy beach, it was difficult for one to land a boat, so dense was the uninterrupted natural vegetation along the shorelines such as here at North Pond.

SWIMMING AT SOUTH POND. Summertime for much of Maine's rural population at the turn of the century was an especially happy respite after the rigors of long winters and short springs. Despite the many demands made upon farm folk in summer, most eked out time here and there for some fun and relaxation such as this spontaneous frolic at the Sandbar in South Pond near Locke's Mills. The obvious fact the children did not have bathing suits with them did not deter them from jumping in clothes and all. And after all, it is just a mile back up to Bird Hill and the farm. Then, too, on a hot summer's day, wet clothes quickly dry. The women were wearing what were called swim dresses.

Nettie, who appears to be teasing Earle, seems to be the only dry one in the group. She evidently set the camera up on the beach and had someone snap the shutter.

From left to right are Winnie, Walter, May Farrington, her daughter Ruth, Earle, Nettie, and Ruby Smith—a local school teacher. May Farrington's husband was Earl Farrington, the field boss at the Maxim Farm during the berry-picking season. It is highly doubtful that he, Howard, or even Moses could spare the time from the farm for such a lark. But come a rainy day, even they might descend Bird Hill in a horse and buggy with their fishing rods to wet a line in Alder River or troll out on South, Round, or North Pond in hopes of bringing back a string of fish for supper.

NORTH POND, SOUTH FROM DUDLEY COTTAGE. In addition to farms such as Mid-Mountain Farm on Bird Hill, inns such as Dudley Cottage and much more grandiose hotels were built on the summits of mountains, hills, and vantage points overlooking scenic bodies of water before the turn of the century. Most inns, even several miles from a body of water, maintained a bath and boat house on the shore of some lake or pond, accessible by a horse-drawn conveyance. Some, of course, were within easy walking distance to the water's edge.

Summer visitors could readily reach Locke's Mills from out of state by taking the Boston and Maine Railroad to Portland and then the Grand Trunk inland to Locke's Mills, Bethel, New Hampshire, Vermont, and even into Canada.

ISLAND COTTAGE GROUP (1905). A group of young ladies, including familiar faces from Bird Hill, relax on the veranda at Island Cottage on one of the islands on North Pond.

Shortly before the turn of the century a few summer people from away had built cottages, usually quite rustic and blending in very nicely with their wooded surroundings, on one of the three local ponds. There were also a sprinkling of cottages owned by wealthier locals in the Oxford Hills area such as the owners of Island Cottage. From left to right are Celia Estes, Annie Crooker, Rena George, and Nina Bean.

DUDLEY COTTAGE. Dudley Inn, as it was frequently called by summer people, was a typical turn-of-the-century summer resort, offering its guests clean, airy rooms, an immaculate dining room serving mostly locally produced food (including milk, cream, butter, eggs, vegetables, and some fruit), good scenery, and various activities. The same people, usually families, came each summer for their entire vacation. Dudley Inn burned in 1927. By the next decade, inns and hotels declined in popularity.

NORTH POND FROM DUDLEY COTTAGE VERANDA (1907). Nettie took this splendid view in 1907 of North Pond from the veranda of the inn. Interestingly, some summer people tried without success to change the name of North Pond to Dudley Lake.

NORTH POND (1907). Nettie captured everything but the rhythmic sound of gentle waves lapping the pond's wooded shore when she took this photograph of a portion of North Pond with Mt. Abram in the distant background.

DUDLEY COTTAGE (1907). Dudley Cottage with its marvelous bucolic setting—its lovely stonewalls, fields, and orchard—provided its guests with a halcyon retreat "Far from the Madding Crowd." Surely it must have been a working farm before it became an inn.

WADING AT THE SANDBAR (1905). Nettie exemplified the quintessence of summertime when she photographed this carefree trio—Bertha Stevens, Celia Estes, and Rena George—wading in the water at the Sandbar on South Pond during a summer outing.

SUMMER INTERLUDE (1905). Bertha, Celia, and Rena—all about twenty years old in 1905—sit on a piece of driftwood at the edge of the Sandbar at South Pond, letting the miniature waves caress their feet. Their smiling faces exude happiness—happiness in their close friendship and perhaps in sharing their hopes and dreams. Summertime generates optimism. Nettie was adept at creating casual and blithesome scenes.

CELIA AT THE SANDBAR (1905). Celia poses for her aunt, standing alone on a driftwood log that was cast up on the edge of the Sandbar at South Pond. She is wearing a typical swim dress or bathing suit of the day.

CELIA AT THE SANDBAR. Celia stands above her ankles in the clear water at the Sandbar, shading her eyes as if attempting to observe something out on South Pond or on the far shore. In all these scenes, taken apparently in a single day at South Pond in 1905, Nettie must have positioned herself and her camera a few feet off shore either in the water or on a boat or float of some sort.

BEAVER DAM, ROUND POND. The remains of a beaver dam and old floating logs rendered this narrow portion of Round Pond nearly impassible when Nettie took this photograph of the dense, wooded shoreline casting its dark reflection into the mirror-like waters. Few things are more startling on such a quiet stream then the sudden resounding whack of a beaver's tail against the surface of the water.

OUT FOR A ROW ON ROUND POND. Sometime between 1906 and 1908 Nettie photographed the Rand children, Ralph and Elsie, in this square stern rowboat on Round Pond. The Rand family were summer residents.

Boating and canoeing on Maine's innumerable lakes, ponds, and streams were favorite summertime activities, even before the turn of the century, for both summer residents and the "natives."

FISHING ON SOUTH POND. Earle and his uncle Gene are enjoying a day of fishing out on South Pond. Uncle Gene appears to be playing in a fish on his fly rod.

INDIAN POND (1905–10). Nettie traveled several miles from Bird Hill to an area in Greenwood called the Bryant Neighborhood to photograph basin-like Indian Pond outlined by dark forestal hills and fluffy white clouds floating overhead.

E•TING WATERMELON. Summertime was watermelon time, especially on the Fourth of July. Frances Cummings, her cousin Earle, and her sister Florence are obviously savoring every mouthful of what was at the turn of the century a special treat for most rural Maine youngsters. A fast-maturing watermelon, however, would soon hereafter be developed that would grow in Maine.

CAPTAIN JONES AND CREW (1907). Captain Jones sits in the bow paddling a boat of local young people on North Pond. Facing him from stern to bow are Florence Cummings, Lura Bradbury (on his left), Walter Maxim (on his right), and Winnie and Earle seated in the stern seat. Captain Jones was married to Moses' sister Abby. The couple adopted Moses' son Gene, after his mother died in 1863.

ALDER RIVER MILL POND (1905–07). What an absolutely picturesque scene! The Alder River School—or Locke's Mills School as it was called until the new school was built in 1890—sat on the very edge of the mill pond. This one-room school was later purchased by E.L. Tebbets as a company rent. Nettie attended school here after the closure of the Bird Hill School. On a hot day in May, the teacher must have had his/her hands full trying to keep the youngsters out of the water or from straying off to fish.

JOHNNY'S BRIDGE (1907). An unidentified couple is about to row under Johnny's Bridge, arching over Alder River, to enter the river from North Pond.

ELSIE RAND (*c.* 1908). Petite and sprightly Else Rand, dressed in summer finery and sporting a fancy parasol to match, stands next to a stately red pine tree near the edge of Round Pond. The Rands probably came from the Lisbon area.

It was not uncommon for summer people and the local residents to interact; and oftentimes enduring friendships (although usually a bit paternalistic) developed. Many of the "natives" earned an important portion of their annual income working for summer residents as caretakers, guides, and domestics. The summer people also were a ready market for locally grown and raised farm produce.

Eight
Barn Cats

THREE KITTENS IN A BASKET (1906). Leave a box or a basket around, and there will soon be a furry feline curled comfortably in it having a snooze. These three adorable kittens remain wide awake, and what photographer could resist taking their picture?

Nettie always referred to her cats as "barn cats," but from many of her photographs, it appears that they were cradled and loved and must have had the run of the house.

WINNIE AND CAT (1906). No one in the Maxim family adored cats more than Winnie. Her mother took this portrait of her daughter at the age of ten cuddling her favorite cat named Jack.

Winnie had a lifelong love affair with cats, and at the age of ninety-two she was photographed in her kitchen at her home in North Bridgton with her favorite cat. When she gave up housekeeping and went to a nursing home in Bridgton, she was accompanied by her cat named Lady Gray.

WALTER MAXIM AND CAT (1906). Then it apparently was Walter's turn to pose with Jack the cat, one of the family's all-time favorite cats, whose name has filtered down through all these many years and was fondly recalled by both Winnie and Walter right up to their recent deaths. Walter, whose outfit is an interesting study in itself, was nine years old when this portrait was taken.

KITTENS: BESS AND TED (1907). As she did with people, Nettie obviously had a knack for getting cats and especially her kittens to strike irresistible poses. She also developed considerable skill using light with a minimum amount of equipment. Both kittens, diversely marked from each other, are beautifully illuminated.

THREE KITTENS IN A BASKET (1906). A pyramid of kittens more than fills this berry basket.

JACK THE CAT (May 1907). Jack the cat, reclining regally on a doily and sofa pillow like an Ottoman sultan, bears little resemblance to a barn cat in this photograph.

Cats were an integral part of practically every farm in rural Maine before and after the turn of the century. Most of them were truly barn cats, with only the family favorites allowed into the house. Barn cats were meant to keep the rodent population under control; but another problem commonly arose—the cat population all too frequently exploded, and trying to control it was about as easy as monitoring the rural population of China.

Most barn cats were well fed, especially wherever there were cows. Twice a day at milking time, the barn cats would converge upon the tie-up and sit—usually as stoically as Buddhas—either waiting for their saucers or pans to be filled with warm, foamy milk right from the cow, or for the milker to test his aim by intermittently squirting a teat full of milk into their open mouths. This little sport helped to ease the ennui of milking.

KITTENS: BESS AND TED (1907). What an incredible shot! One wonders how Nettie managed to get these two adorable kittens to look simultaneously directly up into her lens long enough to take this extraordinary shot. Possibly she had Winnie or someone else holding their attention long enough for her to focus and squeeze the bellows. Cat photography can be both fun and a challenge. Clearly Nettie took great delight in arranging and photographing the family cats and kittens, and unquestionably she was equal to the challenge.

96

HENRIETTA CUMMINGS MAXIM.
Henrietta, Howard's mother, is the
center of attention as she feeds one cat
while two others await their turns.
This is one of the few extant Nettie
Maxim photographs of her mother-in-
law.

WINNIE SITTING WITH THOMAS
(1901). All that is missing in this portrait
of five-year-old Winnie tenderly holding
Thomas in her lap is the sound of
Thomas purring contentedly. Nettie
really captured a very precious moment
in time with this photograph.

BESS IN HAT (November 1, 1907). Little Bess peering over the rim of a bowler is a fitting conclusion to a very special Nettie Maxim series, which accentuates the versatility of this young farmer's wife as a photographer.

Nine
Flowers

PANSIES. At some point during the last decade of her life, Nettie artistically arranged this array of smiling pansies for interior still life photography. Flowers were a favorite subject for artists and photographers around the turn of the century. Certainly Nettie had an abiding love for both wild and cultivated flowers and often sketched them before she took up photography. On the flyleaf of her algebra book for the fall term in 1891 at Gould Academy in Bethel, she drew a very impressive stylized, floriated pen-and-ink drawing (see p. 6).

WINNIE AND ROSE BUSH (June 1908). Winnie, like her mother, had a lasting love for flowers. With a rose and a ribbon in her hair and a stylish long dress that Nettie very likely designed and made, Winnie—at the age of twelve—sniffs a perfumed rose from a bush higher than her head. Interestingly this is the only photograph in this collection showing her wearing glasses.

ROSES. A fallen rose from the bud vase casts a subtle reflection upon the polished, finely-grained wooden surface of a table.

FLOWER ARRANGEMENT. A bouquet of mayflowers or trailing arbutus attractively arranged brought joy and fragrance into rural homes in early May, for almost as soon as the snow melts in the Maine woods and where fields and trees merge, the dainty little white and pink mayflowers begin to bloom.

A very old tradition, especially in rural Maine, that was certainly popular at the turn of the century and still lingers in some rural areas, is the hanging of May baskets, containing a bouquet of mayflowers and perhaps a small gift. Usually the basket was hung surreptitiously on the doorknob or in front of the door of some friend or sweetheart. If the person hanging the May basket was detected, then the recipient would attempt to catch and reward him/her with an embrace and very often a kiss. What young man would not want to be caught by a pretty girl? But then, few young ladies really wanted to escape the clutches of their favorite "bos."

101

LADY SLIPPERS. A carefully-arranged canvas backdrop augments the aesthetic beauty of this trio of graceful pink lady slippers, almost certain to be growing in their natural habitat.

LADY SLIPPERS. This simple arrangement of pink lady slippers in what appears to be an ordinary drinking glass is actually quite effective.

Even before the last patches of sullied snow vanish, the woods and meadows in rural Maine become renascent with spring bloom. The abundance of such wild flowers as the lady slipper in Nettie's day did not suggest the eventual need to protect them.

GLADIOLI. Tall, graceful multiflorous gladioli, the orchids of the Temperate Zone, are perfect subjects for close-up vertical still life paintings or photographs.

GLADIOLUS. As it continues to be today, the gladiolus at the turn of the century was one of the most popular flowers to be cultivated—especially for bouquets to embellish the interior of both rural and urban homes, churches, exhibitions at fairs, grange halls, and countless other public and private places. Their dazzling and exotic array of colors in late summer and early fall lent an aura of the tropics to the North Country, until inevitably the icy fingers of a heavy frost abruptly transformed yards and gardens into wastelands. It was then that all-too-brief euphorias gave way to the harsh realities of what lay ahead, especially for those who lived on hill farms such as on Bird Hill.

FLORENCE CUMMINGS (*c.* 1906). Although Florence Cummings was self-conscious about her plainness and felt that her younger sister Frances was much more attractive and photogenic, Aunt Nettie surely must have enhanced her self-esteem with this photographic arrangement in which she is almost regally attired and nearly surrounded by roses. Roses have a way of touching the very depths of one's inner soul with beauty, and very likely this young fifteen-year-old, for a moment or two early in July when the rose bushes in rural Maine usually have reached the zenith of florescence, felt like Cinderella.

POND LILIES. Nettie very likely knew little of Asian culture, but surprisingly she manifested the skills of one well-schooled in the art of Japanese flower arrangement with this superb and Zen-like arrangement of white pond lilies. The simplistic beauty of this still life releases the tension and relaxes both body and soul.

TIGER LILY. Wild or domestic, tiger lilies lend a touch of opulence to rural Maine roadsides and dooryards in late July. Here in this fine close-up they look majestic towering above the rustic rail fence and staring earthward. This is actually an "Oriental" lily.

CELIA ESTES, APPLE BLOSSOMS (June 1904). For folks living at the turn of the century among the hills of rural Maine, apple blossom time was truly what the monsoons are to people in India—a time of great auspiciousness and joy. The long winter and early spring hiatus was but another memory. It was a time when optimism was at its apex. One's hopes and dreams, especially of young people like Celia, were soaring higher and higher as the trees grew heavier with aromatic blossoms. It was also the time of year when each farm bristled with activity. Aspirations for a cornucopian harvest were never greater.

APPLE BLOSSOMS (1902–03). Ruth Farrington and Winnie Maxim are the very avatars of innocence beneath a myriad of apple blossoms. This is a precious moment in time that Nettie recorded with her camera. These two little girls, so carefree, so unburdened with the vicissitudes of life, belonged to a world that moved at a much slower pace, one that was more self-contained. Like the apple blossoms, it was a world destined to be evanescent.

Ten
Locke's Mills

BANDSTAND, LOCKE'S MILLS COMMON. Sometime during her abbreviated photographic career, Nettie took this tranquil view of a portion of the village of Locke's Mills with Mt. Abram in the distance, and it was made into commercial postcards.

At one time almost every village displayed a bandstand where the local band gave concerts on special occasions. This lovely little stand was moved here from behind the railroad station across the bridge spanning the Little Androscoggin. Unfortunately over-zealous revelers, celebrating the end of World War I in 1919, set it on fire. It was replaced by the Veteran's Honor Roll.

GREENWOOD ROAD (JULY 18, 1909). At the turn of the century the Greenwood Road, passing by South Pond about 1 1/2 miles from the village of Locke's Mills, was not much wider than the road up Bird Hill.

Although, as has previously been pointed out, Bird Hill was in the town of Bethel, the road down the hill from the Cummings-Maxim Farm led directly to the bustling village of Locke's Mills in the town of Greenwood—first settled in 1802 and incorporated in 1816.

Central to the village in Nettie's day were the Tebbets Manufacturing Company (that manufactured sundry kinds of wood products such as spools), the Long Lumber Mill, a grist mill, a post office, a variety of stores, repair shops, and a school that provided education for the children on Bird Hill once the local school up there was closed. Locke's Mills was a mercantile center, a service center, an educational center, and a source of employment for Bird Hill residents—including eventually Howard himself.

But most important of all to the folks on Bird Hill was the Grand Trunk Railroad and the station at Locke's Mills. Without the railroad, Moses and Howard could never have shipped their raspberries and blackberries to Portland and beyond. The same can be said for their surplus milk, cream, butter, and other farm produce. On occasions when Nettie and other members of the family and neighbors had the time and the resources to travel beyond Bird Hill and Locke's Mills, the railroad provided them with the means of getting quickly to their destinations at a time when the only other mode of transportation was by horse and buggy or wagon along meandering dirt roads that at times were impassible even with horses. In short, for the people just a mile or so up Bird Hill, Locke's Mills was a vital link and a window to the outside world.

MAIN STREET, LOCKE'S MILLS. Although dusty Main Street looking west was nearly deserted when Nettie took this photograph around 1906, Locke's Mills was a thriving and dynamic community and must have seemed like a metropolis and an exciting adventure for those who rarely descended Bird Hill.

To the left are the Company Store, the Tebbets Manufacturing Company office, the boiler room and mill, the Old Yellow House (used as a company rent), and the church. To the right is the Tebbets House, the post office, the barber shop, a company house, and a company store.

THE SPOOL MILL (1906–07). As the major employer, the Tebbets Manufacturing Company formed the core of the community of Locke's Mills.

GRIST MILL AT THE DAM. Until after the turn of the century, the miller was nearly as indispensable to every little Maine community as the blacksmith. Wherever there was a stream with water enough to turn a waterwheel, a grist mill was usually set up.

This mill complex with the grist mill to the right and the saw mill to the left was built by Samuel B Locke II in 1842. These new buildings were built several hundred feet down the Alder River from the original site.

Nettie took this photograph before 1899 with her 1-1/2-by-2-inch camera. It is copied and enlarged from one of Nettie's contact prints. The limitations of her first camera are somewhat visible here in the flatness and lack of detail.

MAIN STREET, LOCKE'S MILLS. This is the tree-lined main thoroughfare through Locke's Mills as it appeared around the turn of the century. The first house on the left is today the Greenwood Historical Society, which houses nearly all of Nettie Maxim's glass negatives and photographs.

DANA GRANT HOUSE (1909). This house, owned by Dana Grant, a merchant who operated a store in East Bethel until his retirement, was probably built originally as a mill house in the 1840s.

Nettie was fortunate indeed to capture with her camera Judge Addison E. Herrick seated proudly in his new 1909 two-cylinder Maxwell, manufactured in Tarrytown, New York. Judge Herrick had been a teacher and principal of Blue Hill Academy, as well as a prominent Bethel attorney, state legislator, and county judge. Local historian W.B. Lapham, who referred to him as a self-made man, said of him in his *History of the Town of Bethel* (published in 1891): "He is made of that stuff that never fails of success."

Herrick was born in Greenwood on June 24, 1847, attended Hebron Academy, graduated from Bowdoin College in 1875, and married Mary Chase, the aunt of novelists Mary Ellen Chase and Virginia Chase Perkins. His lovely Queen Anne-style house, built in 1885 on Broad Street in Bethel, survives largely unaltered.

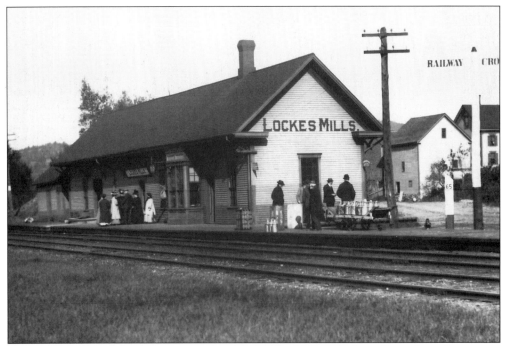

LOCKE'S MILLS RAILROAD STATION. The number of people milling about the station platform awaiting the arrival of the train, as well as the milk cans filled with milk and cream, underscores the importance of the Grand Trunk Railroad and other railroads throughout Maine at the turn of the century.

THE STATION (1907). This driver and team of the Hanover Stage await the arrival of the next train at the Locke's Mills Station. The stage carried passengers destined for Rumford Point and Hanover, 15 miles or so east, along a meandering, dusty East Bethel Road and across the Androscoggin River on the ferry between Rumford Point and Rumford Corner.

MT. ABRAM HOTEL (c. 1906). Even before the scenic waterways, hills, and mountains began attracting summer visitors to the area, the railroad and local industries warranted the building of a hotel. Benjamin Warren Bean, a local farmer and carpenter and the father of Inez and L.L. Bean, built and began operating in 1872 the Mt. Abram Hotel, a replacement for the old Alder River House which had burned. Waiting in front of the hotel is George Tuttle and his stage.

BROADVIEW INN. A decade or so later summer people began arriving by train in rapidly increasing numbers. The Broadview Farm, owned by Sam Felt, was just one of several farms in the area that began catering to summer tourists. Obviously Felt was successful, for as Nettie's photograph indicates, he very rapidly converted his farm into a sprawling inn. It was destroyed by fire around 1917.

CHURCH (1908). The small churches such as this 1883 Union Church in Locke's Mills were a vital part of every rural Maine community at the turn of the century. Nettie and her family descended Bird Hill to worship here, and Nettie, Howard, Moses, Juliette, and Earle (who died in France) are all buried here in the Mt. Abram Cemetery, which was laid out by Samuel Locke II, his brother Dr. John Locke, W.B. Lapham, and Dr. D.W. Davis.

MOSES HOUGHTON HOUSE (1906). In 1856 Moses Houghton bought out Samuel B. Locke II and built this house. In 1906, when Nettie took this picture, Charles and Mary Bartlett lived here. Charles was manager of the Mt. Abram Hotel. Mary can be seen sitting on the front steps of the house.

LOWER MAIN STREET (1909). Elm-shaded lower Main Street in Locke's Mills differed little from the main streets of scores of other small towns and villages throughout Maine in the early 1900s. Board sidewalks were especially convenient during mud season.

WILLIAM COLLIDGE HOUSE. It is thought that this house on lower Main Street was built around 1840 as a mill house. When Nettie took this photograph, however, it was the home of the Collidge family. Standing against the tree is William Collidge, the local blacksmith. Also in the photograph is his wife Hanna, who taught school, and Will Jr., holding the horse. Little Will later ran away and never returned. He eventually purchased a farm in the town of Poland.

FANNIE LITTLEFIELD & DAUGHTER ESTHER. Fannie Littlefield posed with her youngest of three children for Nettie, c. 1907. Fannie was married to Clinton Littlefield, a farmer and house painter who owned a teahouse at North Pond, a dance hall, and Littlefield's Beach at South Pond.

Nettie's skill as portrait photographer obviously was in some demand down at Locke's Mills. It is not known whether she was paid for her work or did it gratuitously for friends and acquaintances in the village and the surrounding area.

EARL & MAY FARRINGTON'S HOUSE. Earl Farrington, who was the field boss at the Maxim Farm on Bird Hill during the berry-picking season, lived here with his family when Nettie took this photograph.

The house was built in 1850 by Isaac Grant (father of Dana). Afterward it passed to several generations of daughters. When the Atlantic & St. Lawrence Railroad (Grand Trunk) was being built in 1851–52, the downstairs was rented to railroad workers.

This photograph of the Farrington Place is a good example of Nettie's artistry and fine composition, especially when photographing farm buildings.

RUTH FARRINGTON & RUTH STOWELL (1908). These two Locke's Mills belles are very stylishly dressed for their portraits. Shortly after the turn of the century it had become fashionable for young girls to wear dresses and skirts just 2 or 3 inches below the knee. Ruth Stowell's father was Charles E. Stowell, proprietor of a local general store and the post office.

FAIRBANKS FAMILY (1904–05). Family traditions were strong throughout rural Maine at the turn of the century and families gathered whenever possible. Nettie was the photographer for this Fairbanks family gathering.

Shown are, from left to right: (front row) Maude (Fairbanks) Lapham and Emma O. Fairbanks; (middle) Carlton Lapham; (back row) Mark K. Lapham, Cleve Fairbanks, and Joe Fairbanks. Joe and Mark worked at the Tebbets Manufacturing Company.

Eleven

Beyond Bird Hill

COUNTY BUILDINGS, SOUTH PARIS. In 1895, the same year that Nettie took up photography, the county seat of Oxford was moved down from Paris Hill to South Paris, mainly because the railroad had been laid through South Paris.

It was only on rare occasions that Nettie traveled beyond Locke's Mills and even rarer that she left Oxford County, which had been a part of Cumberland County until 1805. There is no real evidence that she ever left the state of Maine. Her world was indeed a microcosm. What worldly knowledge she possessed was acquired from the outside world filtering into Locke's Mills and Bird Hill via the railroad through books, newspapers, magazines, and summer visitors.

MOTHER'S BIRTHPLACE. At some point shortly after the turn of the century Nettie traveled by the Hanover Stage, very likely with her mother, to visit and photograph the farm at Rumford Point where Juliette Barker Cummings was born—less than 15 miles from Bird Hill. As Nettie's view of the farm and its surroundings indicate, it was archetypical of nineteenth-century Maine farms, especially throughout the hinterland.

RUMFORD FALLS (Autumn 1904). It was probably while visiting her mother's farm that she photographed the Androscoggin River thundering over Rumford Falls on its way to the Atlantic Ocean.

RUMFORD FALLS (Autumn 1904). Nettie very likely was filled with mixed emotions as she photographed the spectacle of the swirling waters of the Androscoggin and the sprawling paper mill with its minaret-like stacks belching smoke and a foul odor skyward.

ALLIE AND EMILY KEYES (May 24, 1903). On a pleasant day in May when the North Country had once again fully awakened from a long and deep winter's sleep, the Keyes—dressed in their finery—went for a leisurely drive on a tree-shaded road that followed along the banks of the Androscoggin. Allie Keyes was related to the first settlers of Rumford.

BETHEL COMMON (1909). Even though Bird Hill was in the town of Bethel, Nettie had to travel the mile or so down the hill to Locke's Mills and take the "Up Train" to Bethel Village.

The beautiful Bethel Common was donated in the early nineteenth century to the town of Bethel by Captain Eleazer Twitchell, one of the town's founders. About two years after Nettie took this photograph, near Gould Academy which she attended as a teenager, the Prospect Hotel (built in 1861) in the background was destroyed by fire and replaced in 1912 by the imposing Colonial Revival-style Bethel Inn.

BETHEL MONUMENT SQUARE (1909). This classic Civil War monument was erected by the town of Bethel in 1908, about a year before Nettie took this photograph.

ALDER RIVER BRIDGE, BETHEL (1909). The placid waters of the Alder River flow beneath this rude bridge and into the Androscoggin south of Bethel Village on what is today Route 26. The split stone abutments are an enduring testimonial to the magnificent skill and work ethics of Maine's early stone cutters and builders. Of course, the bridge itself was much less durable.

HILDA AND FLORENCE CHAPMAN (1908). The pretty little Chapman sisters, who were born on a hillside farm in Bethel, were probably living at the Woodstock Gore when they posed sedately in matching dresses and necklaces for Nettie.

THE BLACKSMITH. This marvelous photograph of an unidentified blacksmith working at his forge, thought to have been located in East Bethel, is an outstanding example of Nettie's ability to use both artificial and natural light in her photography.

A working blacksmith is extremely challenging to photograph, for he toils only by the light of the fire. Since he monitors the temperature of the metal by the subtle changes in color, working in a dark space is essential.

The blacksmith was indispensable to every town and hamlet throughout rural Maine at the turn of the century. Many farmers who lived in isolated areas such as Bird Hill learned the basics of blacksmithing in order to keep their farms functioning.

ALBANY BASIN FALLS. Nettie had to have traveled by horse and buggy several miles from Bethel to take this highly artistic chiaroscuro photograph of the falls in what is today Albany Plantation. This is an outstanding example of her use of natural light to attain maximum effectiveness. After graduating from Gould Academy, Nettie taught in Albany, not far from these falls.

SCREW AUGER FALLS. To photograph spectacular Screw Auger Falls, Nettie had to travel even further by carriage over devious roads north of Bethel and beyond Newry to Grafton Notch, just south of Upton.

125

PORTLAND HEAD LIGHT. It must have been a highlight in Nettie's abbreviated life to venture all the way to Portland and out to the Portland Head Light, which had been guiding ships safely into Portland Harbor since January 10, 1791. She took full advantage of this excursion to capture this splendid seascape.

VIEW FROM CAPE ELIZABETH. As she watched and photographed this freighter slowly threading its way into Portland Harbor out beyond these menacing emerging megaliths, resembling a school of whales, perhaps a longing to venture across the ocean to some distant land swept over her like waves on the distant shore.

SURF, CAPE ELIZABETH. Nettie virtually captured the sea's powerful rote, as the waves swirl around and break over the protruding rocks. Her encounter with this portion of coastal Maine was brief; it was a world apart from Bird Hill and the susurration of a soft summer breeze sweeping across a sea of grass crested with daisies.

OLD ORCHARD BEACH PIER (1906). A trip to Old Orchard Beach meant simply taking the Grand Trunk from Locke's Mills to Portland and transferring to the Boston & Maine for the short trip to Old Orchard. It was quicker and easier than traveling the few miles to such places north of Bird Hill as Grafton Notch. Nettie's photograph of the famous Old Orchard Pier was taken just a few years after the rebuilding of Herbert Hildreth's original "Golden Mile" in 1898.

POND SHORE ROAD (October 1909). The real world of Nettie Cummings Maxim was far inland and far beyond the crescendo of a storm-tossed sea and the mewing of gulls planing against a windswept sky. Her world was the narrow wooded roads—such as here at the Woodstock Gore—where graceful young birches, like gymnasts, arch over the still waters of North Pond, and the only sounds might have been the luffing of a gentle wind through autumn leaves, the glissando of a wood thrush deep inside the woods, and the purling of a brook tumbling toward the pond. It was a perfect place and time for reflecting. Unfortunately, Nettie was viewing the last autumn of her life. Come next May she would be taking her last journey down Bird Hill—to rest in the Mt. Abram Cemetery in Locke's Mills.